DIVIDING
UNTANGLED
LIGHT

Verses of the Finite Heart

DIVIDING UNTANGLED LIGHT

Verses of the Finite Heart

A Poetry Collection

by

EUFE TANTIA JR.

Illustrations by

Zephanie Estelle Tantia

Zacharie Ervine Tantia

VINE & STELLE
Publications

Dividing Untangled Light: Verses of the Finite Heart

ISBN-13: 979-8-9938478-0-1 (Paperback)

ISBN-13: 979-8-9938478-1-8 (Hardcover case wrap)

ISBN-13: 979-8-9938478-2-5 (E-Book - EPUB)

ISBN-13: 979-8-9938478-3-2 (Hardcover Dust Jacket)

Library of Congress Control Number: 2025925790

Illustrations: Zephanie Estelle Tantia and Zacharie Ervine Tantia.

Editing, cover design, and photographs: Eufe Tantia Jr.

Cover design created with Canva.

Published by Vine and Stelle Publications.

Seminole, Texas

United States of America.

For my Rose,
Zach, and Zelle,
who appreciate the art and power
of language and love.

To the Almighty,
the Source of all blessings.

Contents

"The world is full of poetry. The air is living with its spirit;
and the waves dance to the music of its melodies, and
sparkle in its brightness."

— James Gates Percival

"'Hope' is the thing with feathers –
That perches in the soul –
And sings the tune without the words –
And never stops – at all –"

— Emily Dickinson

TO THE READER

Dividing Untangled Light: Verses of the Finite Heart
contemplates the human yearning for light—love,
hope, and spiritual clarity—as we travel through
life's gorge of shadows and starlight. This light is
universal, though not always visible. It boldly
sparkles in the assuring love songs of a sunny
morning, shyly flickers in the enveloping reality of
dusk, and gently shines from the guiding star in the
serene night. Yet, the finite mind and heart can only
appreciate the visible spectrum by unraveling each
wavelength, each color, and splitting each light
strand into finer threads.

To help me make sense of this, I turned to allegory,
conceit, and metaphor and shaped into poetry these
divided strands of light. My verses explore themes as
varied as unrequited and fulfilled love, parenthood,
grief and loss, faith, culture, and society. In some
poems, I lamented the swift passing of time and the
transience of life, and in others, I examined the

heart's aspirations for spiritual growth, balance, and healing. The underlying theme of Divine influence and guidance is woven throughout the book, offering true hope amid human experience.

Although I arranged these reflections and refractions as a purposeful journey, feel free to start with any poem that resonates with you. Ultimately, I hope that you use these verses as a lens (or, perhaps, a prism) and not merely a mirror. Gaze beyond my own perspectives and viewpoints. Within these pages, you may be able to unravel your own distinct and vibrant strands of light.

"Magnificence Behind the Past"

Wyoming, USA

PRELUDE: GRATITUDE FOR LIGHT

Wonders of the daily skies from
simple sunshine to vanishing rainbows,
proof of perfection in power,
engage my seeking mind.

Strange songs of the infinitely deep
heart's jeweled caverns and chasms,
linger on my palms like the digital dew,
fleet beyond my grasping thought.

But, the stars, though light-years away,
the moon, though it waxes and wanes:
these, the Divine gracefully unveils,
these, no more shall shadows eclipse.

Snowy nights and starlit crossroads,

perplexing lakes and forked paths,

lonely isles with serenity's gems,

all beckon me to venture forth.

Broken strands that make me whole,

beaming pillars that draw my heart to shore,

The One is love and light—true, untangled;

here, my journey to explore begins.

Part One

sunshine and song

FÜR MEINE ROSE

What can translate

the love we share?

Is it literature, or art,

or the beating of the heart?

Does it dwell in nature's intricacy?

Can it ride on whimsical melody?

The sleepy scent of a humid rose,

the cryptic songs of obsidian crows,

are forged into a new language: thus—

Looks. Cuddles.

Laughs. Smiles.

These simple things for us mean:

"We write our own lines."

CAPTIVE

You are the Helen to my Paris,

The bluest star that shifts the night,

Unbound by Aion, peerless, ethereal,

A scarlet snowflake in blizzards of white.

In fading forests, under retreating shades,

I wait, a silent deer, beside the thinning stream,

Motionless, fenced in by unyielding Dryads,

I can *only* live love in an eternal dream.

STRANGER

I see you for the first time.
You don't even see me yet.

Instead, you squint at the spark,
not of the sunlight-filtering window,
but of my shining eyes.

I, a stranger to you,
speak your name.
You, a stranger to me,
break into a small cry,
yet your tears hear my voice
without shedding a drop of fear.
Maybe your name, riding on my voice,
is not strange to you at all.

My heart now surges as my mind whispers,

today's another of my happiest;

I must raise a robust tower of memories,

build the sturdiest bridges

for you to safely cross.

Holding you close

to my throbbing heart's core,

afraid my unsteady arms

would suddenly fail—let go,

I feel your trust,

like a young, clasping vine,

stretching from your soul to mine.

I, a stranger to you,

look into *your* gleaming eyes.

You're a stranger to me—

open wet clay,

fragile as strands of wool,

eyes that perceive untangled light I hardly see,

mind never sullied,

body barely clothed—

owning nothing

in this world

but my love.

SEASONAL ROLES

How I long to be soft sunlight
That drapes your vast spring meadows,
Warming within the humblest shrubs
Outshone by flowers and rainbows.

How I wish—when spring's song ends—
To play the cello's solo piece
That calms your busy shorelines
In summer's orchestral breeze.

How I want to be a dancing hue
That blushes your autumn palisades.
I'd frolic through brown forest hills
And waltz with their fiery foliage.

When winter comes to your world

Would I play the dazzling snowflake's role?

I'd rather be an ever-present hearth

To warm your lone, chilled soul.

THINK OF LOVE

*T*hink of Love…

locked antlers of rival stags,

wolf's yearning howl for the moon.

Breathe Love…

old book's earthy scent,

child's sun-soaked hair by noon.

See Love's vibrance,

shy blue violet's scattered growth,

slow-reaching roots of a tree.

Taste its flavors,

dark pistachio truffles,

bitter melon sauteed with honey.

Hear Love's voices,

bellowing, crashing rapids,

quiet clock in steady time.

Touch its essence,

white rabbit's silky fur,

cactus's jolting spine.

Contemplate its wonders:

harmonious toil of bees,

machinations of a life cell,

speed of starlight's journey,

if time was born, will die.

Bathe in Love,

the Earth's silver stream

that flows from the Mount above.

To the desert it brings life;

to dark worlds, gives light.

When hearts and lives are bound—

think of Love.

CRAFT

On a stony beach,

you find a dull steel medallion,

scratched, dented, yet whole,

washed up beside

your locked treasure chest.

Like an ancient pendant

dangling before hesitant eyes,

the steel medallion whispers

a strange, hypnotic pledge:

"Take me—

I shall be yours."

If memory of pain is the only lock

of your *empty*, wooden trove,

then polish the dull medallion's surface,

even reshape it to your will,

but do not cast it aside—

for rarely is diamond enclosed in bonded steel.

Gently pry the steel open,

and, if you can prove there is treasure within,

then send your hollow chest

away, forever,

afloat upon the seas,

and keep the medallion of strong steel

pressed solely

between your trembling knees.

A FINCH'S FEARS

I wish for you to grow

but not a chirp too soon;

Time, the hummingbird, I fear,

can rapidly beat its wings.

I wish for you to fly

to great heights, on your own,

yet I fear to let go until

your feathers can flap their dreams.

I want to raise our brood

on branches sturdy, strong;

should I, myself, fall short—I fear

you'd alight upon false nests.

I hope that you will learn beyond
our tree and all its ways;
I also fear you may glide, too far,
into tainted, corrupted forests.

I'll be the finch who teaches you
to sing Love, the noblest bird-song.
Make the warble I teach your very own,
but don't forget your tutor.

I want you to be guarded
from the preying claws of pain,
but how would clipping your wings
raise their soaring power?

Day, night, I pray—and pray,

for your wisdom, protection,

and all that's good.

Many fears abound, little scout,

yet the joys of raising,

loving you:

To trade them,

I never would.

LITTLE ISLE OF DESTINY

Shout, smile, all oceans!

Rejoice for him, twin stars!

Applaud this sailor, ye seas!

For his eye has gazed on land.

Ahoy! 'Tis not his hoped-for refuge:

Not the marvelous peaks

amid the vast plains.

Not the cloudy peace

nor the thorns scattered

by the mainland of bliss.

He tried to disembark

on Poseidon's shores;

he failed,

swept away by intolerant winds.

After years of blue-green seas,

joy now along scorched sand springs.

Shout and smile,

all the world!

Your sailor claimed the unforeseen:

A little isle of limitless splendor.

Untamed earth beneath yellow skies—

his Destiny!

Farewell to the continent, O sailor!

Farewell to the New World of vanity.

Farewell to bitter life aboard the ship,

to the relentless, capricious seas!

Rejoice!

For no horde of gold

can buy this slight spot he claims.

'Tis his for life! 'Tis his!

This last, little haven

where he can dwell, at last, content—

if only

his wandering dreams

would cease.

CITIZEN OF TODAY

Man of Tomorrow,

do you want the spectacles you wear to show

a blank page in a novel

a katydid camouflaged as a frail leaf

a complacent, mild-mannered citizen

mediocre grayed-out meekness,

so that you won't stand out?

Or do you want them to conceal

a pyramid in the flat desert

a mammoth breaking cubit-deep ice

a person of steel resolve

disruptive blue-and-red justice,

so that you won't be toppled?

INFANTILE HISTORY

When i tasted some honey, ate it in five scoops

honey hated me, then the bees stung

i lost the honey

but a passing rainbow lit up my eyes

next day was unexpectedly, triflingly joyful

until i discovered some candy gems

glimmering in bright colors

when i bit into them my teeth broke

those were hard! fake candy!

i tossed 'em away

grabbed something sweet again

like a salted chocolate wafer

with a tinge of lemon

but i dropped it on the ground

stomped on it, crushed like a bug

finally found organic milk

primal, unsweetened,

purely from almond,

plain, just solidly white

from then on,

i'll drink this milk to regrow my broken teeth

i'll drink this to become

as wise

as a baby

FIRMAMENT

*O*ne more swift descent

would

bring down my walls,

fling wide my gates,

shatter the world like brittle glass.

Yet I would not reach you.

I have seen the Great Arrow.

I know the head's keenness,

the arc's broad reach.

Its power pierces,

but it cannot break this barrier.

I am the waters above—

You, below.

So it is,

unless

both of us resolve

to watch a hundred shifts,

to wait a thousand drifts,

until we see darkness and light

end their wars,

each peacefully taking its rightful place

in this dividing firmament.

"Gorge of Light and Darkness"

Utah, USA

TO THE LADY OF THE AFTER-DAY

*H*ow fair you are! How fair you are!
O lady of the after-day!
As the summer eve lies in grandeur,
your full beauty takes its sway.

Your eyes exude night's meekness
yet charm as does the mystic moon.
Your hair, vast as the enveloping sky,
makes all peering stars swoon.

Your scent sweetens the evening gusts;
your voice reigns over their unheard hiss.
Tender petals are akin to your touch;
your smile flings my heart into bliss.

Of late-night walks and whispered words:

How dear, how resonant the memory

of flowery gardens, under starlit skies

where we speak of love, alone and free.

As the moon gently lays her tender beams

And the night wind chants forth its songs

To you, O lady of the after-day,

To you my heart now belongs.

But farewell now, O lady of the night,

For the dawn is well on its way.

The shadows are fleeing—let us hasten now!

No longer must we here stay.

How fair you were! How fair you were!

O lady that I once knew

It sorely grieves my stricken heart

To bid you now, "Adieu."

WORLDVIEW

*P*reserved inside the kitchen freezer

Neither ice cream nor frozen veggies

Food

Adorning an earth-scented botanical garden

Neither peonies nor forget-me-nots

Flowers

City bustle watched from the Burj Khalifa's top

Neither hometown nor color

Humanity

In arid soil, a seedling seeking rainclouds

Neither myth nor religion

Hope.

THE ROAD TRIP'S LAST STRETCH

Driving on country roads,
always touching the horizon,
mellow hum of tires on the lonely asphalt—
it's therapeutic—

my mind unearths
forgotten treasure

we might spot wayside deer
exploring this bright afternoon,
just hope none crosses the road
    (check my speed)

    that kindergarten field trip
    to the film center when I was four:
    Mom said I had told her I cried
    when Bambi's mother died…

the road is quite paved,

cracked along some points,

but the ride's not bumpy,

daughter and son are on the back seats

    (glance at rearview mirror)

she's asleep

he's looking out the window

maybe

both of them are in dreams

maybe

they won't feel dizzy and vomit...

    when I was eight:

    I threw up behind a corner stool

    while playing hide-and-seek in my aunt's
    home—

    even though I never told her,

    now I know, she knows...

now, a horse-dotted ranch on the left,

spots of grass darkened by shadows of sparse
clouds,

tree shrubs freckling the bright hills on the right

I imagine myself

      roaming an idyllic meadow

      on this hot afternoon,

      rolling down the low hills,

      running across the field

      as Alice did before she entered the rabbit-hole

you'd think

you could actually

      sprint across the flowing knolls—

      mildly warming sunlight shining on your
nape,

      blissful cows mooing from the pasture,

      your arms spread out wide in the air,

      spinning yourself around while

      singing like Maria—

but if

you're over there

you'll be just a speck on the giant hills

panting after a twenty-yard sprint

cheeks sun-blushed in seven minutes,

you'll realize the grass isn't soft as it seems;

bugs hover, snakes crawl,

you'd step on cattle dung

I could stop

to shoot a landscape photo, even just one

but—

I'll do it next time…

fields are now far behind,

road curves up gently

through a low-lying slope,

mountain pass flanked by assemblies of aspen

oh, the woods! they *always* invite

a deeper, dreamier reverie…

      (glance at my wife)

she's on the passenger seat

arms folded, eyes closed

exhausted from this long drive

maybe *one day*…

     I'd hike with her

     in this sunlight-barring forest

     holding her hand

     while we traverse fallen logs

     green breeze kissing our cheeks

     innocent sparrows chirping overhead, and—

our hair graying,

our backs aching,

our knees creaking,

our hearts straining—

NO—let's do it *now!*

let's turn the next right off the empty highway,

into the dirt road—get out of our car and put on the

hiking boots we brought but never wore for this
trip,

and explore the trails and venture into the green

unknown

but

the amber sun rests straight ahead,

we might get caught by night...

still, before us, lies this far stretch of road

ever touching the horizon...

next time...

next time...

but when?

do what I want on a road trip

next time…

for now,

I'll just drive on toward the sunset—

it's therapeutic.

Part Two

shadows and starkness

FINDING CALLIOPE

*I*n my foolish youth,

I missed our first encounter:

illness veiled my face, restraining

my greeting of your grace. I lost the day

when I might have learned to blend

inspiration with free thought.

yet, I searched for you

perhaps

seized but a whiff of your evanescent balm

listened for traces of your subdued voice

my steps wavered

on slippery stepping stones

as I crossed Time's devious river

and I still revered you,

breathed

your dying candle fumes

heeded

your inaudible breaths

wrought your remnant gifts into cryptic words

seen by none

then I drifted away and wandered,

carrying but an ember of dreams.

now,

where do I find you —

ages past?

in a lonely library row?

in a bereaved bookshop nook?

on a dusty shelf-top, mold-ridden by insignificance

cobwebbed by yesterday in the mind's ancestral
home?

I barely sense

your faded spirit

on today's slick, slender, saturated scrolls...

there, the Muses fall to ruin:

their swiftly fleeing figures struck down

by viciously swifter arrows

by the whirling blades of scythed chariots

forged by soulless man-mimicking smiths,

their light, nimble feet swept under

by false messengers

by Machiavellian aftershocks

by hate-filled cacophony,

their once-rousing voices

now subdued, utterly crushed

by the Furies' strangling hands.

TIN CAN'T

Can't do anything not done

Can't undo something that's done

Can't share my crazy, even cozy dreams

'Cause I'm out of them.

Can't be a devoted dog

Can't be a cynical sage

Can't bleed my heart's blood onto the ground

'Cause I don't have one.

Can't dissect a wicked mind

Can't click my heels to go home

Can only stay a tin man and rust

'Cause I'm afraid to believe.

A FINAL FANTASY

Another item to hoard,
A catch from the digital stream,
The inventory just keeps growing,
No time to consume them all.

Can I conquer more tomes
Absorbing insight from realms?
Not all scrolls are worth reading;
Which books stand the test of time?

Side-quests of sport, music, poetry,
Where skill-tree growth ignites creativity;
Recreation I can only cultivate and enjoy
If brief life fragments are devoted to these.

To grind for gold, in order to thrive,

Ranking up within my job class and guild,

I'm chore-overpowered, tomorrow-investing,

Each day crafting the same bitter potions.

I'm trapped in a role-playing game:

    Quest-juggling,

    Ultimate-hunting,

    Experience-grinding,

    Skill-training,

    Treasure-farming.

With a growing list of to-dos

In my crowded, muddled mind,

Which tasks are worth my finite time?

What mage can clone my time?

For journeys I dream up

On world maps yet unexplored,

I cannot befriend each NPC,

Nor wander every lighted city.

For myself, too, I need time, my own,

To restore health, armor, spirit.

I plead to strengthen links to the Source—

As the orbs can slow no longer.

Family and loved ones—Quests never to bypass,

Casting buffs on the party, healing them with care.

Hours cannot be saved, only delicately balanced.

If I could reload time to gain moments with them!

My life is like a role-playing game:

I wish to explore every dungeon,

I aspire to reach completion.

But maxing out is just a fantasy—

THE FINAL BOSS FIGHT AWAITS

No save points.

No respawn.

No time to experience all things,

No time to do it all,

In one level,

In one act,

In one lifetime.

TRAPPED

When Lyric is shackled by Truth:

It is enclosed by walls

higher than it can scale;

its spirit wails in agony,

for affection can

never again freely flow

with

                    Music.

And the poisons of repression and rebellion

seethe in the silence,

seeping deeper into Lyric's cell,

until they turn the prisoner into stone—

rough, cold on the outside,

forever burning within.

UNHEARD (WHILE MY HEART BEATS)

*L*isten.

My silent heart

turns sluggish

(*bradycardia*)

while your heart

speaks

a new beat.

Can you sense

the unheard murmur

within my walls?

Is my unpredictable language

(*arrhythmia*)

intricate as the nephron's tubules?

Is it

enigmatic as the neuron's sparks?

Has your heart

closed its heavy valves

to shut out fresh blood?

Reach into each chamber,

grasp the burden of my bursting heart

bring your own heart closer

as you listen to my

echoes,

and tell me you hear my life's flow—

You do not.

Then you will never know

the unheard

T

R

U

T

H

that blocks the arteries of my

still,

now

lifeless heart

(asystole)

THE MAGIC POT

$\mathcal{B}$ehold, a magic cooking pot!

It summons any dish you wish.

Whisper the incantation; smoke appears,

hovering above the brim.

Before you utter your desire,

  it already knows your craving.

Mumble that you're *not* starving,

  yet it senses the belly's emptiness.

Brag that you have *no* appetite,

  and it fills your soul with gluttony.

Yet, the pot won't cook your meal until

you add a pinch of salt from your tears.

And when it boils, the savory scent of hot broth

  makes you hunger even for the next feast

  which will require

three drops of your blood—

and the one after that

will always demand more.

AQUARIUM

*B*ig fish,

I'm feeding you again today

always along with the little ones.

I drop the food

into the lighted water,

knowing you'll take them all.

My palm is full of pellets,

enough for every fin,

yet you rush to the surface, swiftly,

to gulp down *every* bit.

You don't remember that you were,

as they are now, once little;

now, you smugly swim around,

flaunting long, ostentatious tails

that sideswipe your poor brethren.

Your greedy bellies swell

like bursting bags of flour.

Your grotesque pop-eyes glaze with greed,

always searching for more.

Let the frail, little guppies and their tinier young

eat just enough to live!

You nip their tails

and gobble their fry

when I withhold your daily feed.

You'll all choke in this same toxic water

if I drop much more than you need.

Little fish,

I'm sorry, I cannot move the big ones

to an isolated tank—

they'll die and decay,

shocked by the cold clarity

of a strange, tranquil world.

You must learn to snatch for yourselves

each scattered crumble of hope

that hasn't yet been devoured.

EVAN JAMES PRUNES A GARDEN

*T*here once was a man named Evan James

Who stumbled upon a ruined garden

Sprawling with tangled thorns

And scarlet, large-eyed beetles,

Ground ivy—purple-green, creeping—

Exhaling the dead earth's stench.

Amid the weedy garden sprouted

Ferns and azaleas, snapdragons and succulents,

And a bed of white lilies cornered by daisies.

Hands clasped to neck, Evan wondered deep:

Who owns the plot? Where is the gardener?

What design was destined for this?

He spotted the bed of tender, little lilies,

White petals—delightful—but starting to brown,

Budding, still glowing, but silently gasping,

Wrestling with the titans for a scrap of sun.

For the garden's sake, Evan James resolved,

I will tend these first-growers, care for no other!

And he took up the gritty, arduous labor

No one else dared to start.

With a spade, he purged growth

And blooms he found unseemly.

With a hoe he slowly raked away

Stubborn weeds causing pain.

He tilled and watered the hardened soil,

Saving the roots' costly freedom and space.

Guided by an ancient gardening book

He found abandoned on a mound of leaves,

Evan James restored the chaotic plot

To a simple, orderly patch.

He rebuilt gray crumbling walls around,

A high refuge for the week's end,

Beyond the reach of slugs and snails,

Feet high above the ground.

From his hallowed, lofty perch above,

He could see the Eden he revived.

After all his effort, he asked himself,

Would the gardener have approved?

With no one to answer, he himself declared,

"This is how it was meant to be!

Who here can continue my scrupulous toil?

I have restored the garden's beauty!"

At the sound of Evan James's voice,

The tenacious ivy stirred,

Slithering insidiously across the soil.

Creeping, burying,

Crawling, constricting,

Till its tendrilled arms reached the high wall's plinth…

It climbed the gray bricks,

Clutched Evan James' leg—

And flung him from his perch.

MONUMENTAL FAULTS

*W*hy the second stone column is cracked,

the fourth twisted,

the architectural order misplaced,

while the building plans

were explicit

why faux windows were added,

surrounded by

bizarre adornments,

not one letting in any light

why there are fifty-nine pristine, pearly stairs

ascending nowhere,

flanked by seven lamps,

lifeless—

> *These, I cannot understand,*
> *I cannot embrace—*

when this carved Colossus,

centuries-old,

vast and overarching,

plated in flaking gold,

salt-bleached and towering from the coast,

claims all its ten columns

were built per the plan,

boasts its ability

to bear its own astonishing weight,

and yet it still draws a thousand ships

to its fractured, faulty base!

Well, then:

How can I judge such a grandiosity?

See my own edifice

surrounded by dusk

on the same impermanent sands.

I, by my merits,

cannot raise even three or four

of my flimsy tide-soaked planks

to brace my ephemeral monument,

now crumbling to watery ground,

where creaking poles meet

the crashing, ominous tide of what is to come.

THE RECITAL

*f*ingers resting on the keyboard,

spine straight, palms curved,

I count, I breathe, to be one with the piano.

I strike the first key, the music begins,

hands grind out the tune as I was taught:

bumping the restrained rhythm with my left hand,

stitching the metered melody with the right.

This isn't me—it's not my signature piece.

My raised wrists feel tautly tied

to only two octaves.

Seriously? Genius and faith must scale

higher than the score!

Completing the subdued, abrupt coda

of this abridged tune,

I refrain from playing

more notes than permitted.

Then I rise

to face the dissonant chords of applause.

I should bow to them—but, by measure,

I do not.

This never was my performance.

DIVIDER

I gave you this two-edged blade,

forged to cleave the most impenetrable granite.

Its solemn scabbard guards the wearer

from mortal harm; incorruptible steel

shines in the darkest oppressive night.

Let Camelot live, O King.

Better to sheath the sword in stone,

for common folk

to grasp, to study,

than to polish its hilt with hubris

and shatter the Round Table's glory!

You injudiciously slew

your own gallant shields,

who, although divided in ideals,

had remained loyal to the land.

Do you blindly believe that

the strange inscription of the ancients

foretold of your hallowed right?

You—now alone—

even with Excalibur's unbreakable might

shall fall to the onslaught

of the decadent horde of Mordred,

your nearest kin but your most pernicious blight.

Your own soul shall be impaled,

your own heart divided,

by the inexorable glaive of the Black Knight

who abhors

the noble kingdom

and the greatest sword of light.

CHÂTEAU DE CHILLON

At Chillon Castle by Lake Geneva
in the grand realm's golden jubilee,
my audience with the Queen awaited
after nine grinding years.

I was a squire
soon to be knighted,
to be bestowed with esteem.

Her Majesty would task me
to row
the cold, leaden Swiss lake,
to brave
the treacherous Alpine pass,
and to seek,
among a thousand uncharted caves

the legendary edelweiss of healing—

a trial before knighthood,

a token of my worthiness,

my heart's vow of allegiance

unto the famed Queen.

Thus, by the lake I stood,

in full polished silver armor,

awaiting her regal arrival,

gazing at the sun's slow waning.

My noble Queen

never crossed the Continent's breadth

nor sent one word across the Channel.

The promise,

my knighthood,

my quest for honor—

all drowned in the lake

beneath the castle,

where the waters forever imprison

dreams

born too late

in the miasmic depths of indifference.

TO THE LATE DAY

Beyond your appointed hour, O Morn
Did you come, with a pale trace of light
Alas! Your single stray hour
Has taught me to love the Night.

RAISED BY A RAINBOW

I saw a rainbow

cleave the dark clouds,

proclaiming its silent greeting.

My tears, the rain;

my spirits, cold winds.

Color flourished in bursts

upon the wounded sky.

Sunshine warmed me,

drying my sodden rags.

A fresh rush of air

revived my struggling spirit.

From where I stood,

I raised my quivering finger

to touch the splendid spectrum.

While I gazed at the rainbow,

my every heartbeat wished it more life;

my every breath pleaded for more time.

Still, its colors drained.

It sighed its farewell.

Shadows gathered—Silence.

Cold winds.

Rain.

Wounds.

I drop to my hands and knees in the mud,

close my eyes, envision gray clouds.

I search for a sliver of yellow,

a streak of white fluff,

find none in a dream.

The wounded sky, like lightning,

flashes its piercing pain to my every tear.

I crumple

alone

fading against the flurried sheets

as if the rainbow never was.

RAINBOWS AREN'T EVERYTHING

Rainbows aren't everything.
  They define but a
  fragment of the vast sky.
  They're bro-
      ken slivers
  of untangled light   up there
          that float

          for just three daydreams
      and suddenly blend into
          secret scentless strands
              you can't even grip!

Why cry when a rainbow fades?
Aren't there wandering eagles,
    glints on treetops,
        royal peaks crowned with white clouds?
    Isn't the space beyond our blue sky black?

Thus, when I spot a rainbow—

I remind myself that its light must vanish.

Wish still,

if I want,

and swiftly chase the rainbow

                          all the way to its end—

the end I will *never* see—

and I might,

maybe,

find a mirage of gold.

PLAINSONG TRACE

*H*ow will you remember me?
You won't remember me by...

my poems
      useless, enigmatic,
forgotten letters
      empty, stale.

spoken words
      reassuring—hurtful,
digital texts
      eventually disappear.

strained eloquence of an amateur
      noble feat, falling short,
empty prayer in public
      more jinxed than blessed.

a monument photograph

    also shot by countless tourists,

my old profile picture—

    true self? never was.

my name, almost unique

    but shared with Dad,

a birthday, same as eleven thousand others'—

    even dear ones sometimes forget.

and not by...

my fingers squeezing son's nose

    to calm his livid thoughts,

warm hand on daughter's back

    to bring her good dreams

our common constellations, stolen dates,

tub of shared ice cream,

angered love I stirred in you

with stubbornness and pride...

but you will only

remember me by…

the sudden jolt you feel

when you confront

I am not here

at all

anymore

AUTUMN SHADOWS AND STORM-LIGHT

*F*ar, eighty-two miles from life

near a silent, shadowed sanctuary

alone she stood

a friendless oak

low dust whirled like ghosts

brittle leaves

scratched the ground

refusing to touch her feet

thunder bellowed, fields far away

as the sun wearily began its exit

sorrow a steel chain around her neck

her head stayed bowed

as she stared at the shiny tombstone

eyes blankly tracing Sarah's epitaph

memory blew past her:

midnight waves of hair

resting on bony shoulders

warped virtue, petty vileness

bonds like sisters

separation eight autumns apart—*or nine?*

planned reunion in a few days

never again met—

the dusk-crow's shriek

jolted her from trance—

she had stood there

wept there

alone as the

grave

now, hours had passed—*six? four?*

she could not trace

how the day had swiftly abandoned her

for the long, bygone hours

had not been porous enough

to soak up the dawn of her grief

and soon darkness began

to blot out starlight

gusts howled in melody

tree branches waved to the rhythm

a paper-crumpling tumult drew near—

drips

drops

piercing water-shards

struck the earth

ever nearer

sharp lightning blazed

deep thunder

boomed, *crashed*!

the ebony churchyard gate

groaned and swung shut

steel clanging against rusted steel

wet leaves scampered in panic over the ground

wind sought to steal her veiled hat

made her brown skirt dance in waves

a flashing razor

gouged the sky once more

its jagged bolt

revealing

moss-covered stone arches

of the cemetery church

the heavens furiously demanded her retreat
thunder-growling, *"Enough defiance!"*

darkness crept forward;
the night's imminent stare
the elements' screaky chorus
the wind-whispered shadows playing behind her
all quickened her pulse

if only I could escape the turmoil,
find shelter
where? beneath the tree? —
inside the church!

body shaking
cursing water and chill
wishing for day to return
and summer to burn her

she broke from the graveyard

raced the slippery

stones leading to the hallowed fortress:

refuge—at last?

but the once-welcoming haven

had turned into an infernal sanctuary

cackling against the sinister storm-light

that clawed at the impending eve's shroud

she arrived at steps before the

front door

windowed with stained glass

black emptiness beyond its threshold—

should I enter?

rain gushed

while for a minute she stood fixed, frozen

looking beyond the heavy door

she finally

gazed up—shocked reverence

widening her eyes

knocking out her breath—

at the glistening, grim structure

looming over her like a diabolical magistrate

sentencing her to eternal solitude

and as she bent back her head

the cold wind triumphantly snatched away her

drenched mourning hat

sweeping it to the mud-drowned grass

spread on the wayside

she turned, rushed, stooped

to pick up the mud-stained hat

her dark, wind-tangled hair shrouded her face
as if to shield from black and cold

the storm's fading banshee wail
echoed against the dying rainfall—

an icy hand-like touch
brushed against her shoulder,
she let out a gasp
sharp as the lightning's nail,

spun and saw

her own face—

herself, untroubled eyes grayed by grief,
midnight hair serene as frozen moonbeams—
smiling through the storm.

Part Three

serenity and starlight

ANOTHER SNOWFLAKE

I'm watching

another snowflake fall.

Guided by the softest gusts of winter,

it drifts in a slant

to join the deepening snow,

a collective, layered white on the solemn earth.

Each glowing crystal

I have known

once did sustain

the sun-parched grass;

each a drop of vital water

that rose back to the swirling sky,

in a course

that I never pictured broken,

in a season

where one would never turn to ice.

Thawing will come after,

but snowflakes don't know;

they *are* the snow.

We, the raindrops that remain,

awaiting our fated moment

to turn cold and fall,

can only hope

that the spring sun's glory

and reuniting warmth

will arrive any day now.

Indeed, while it still snows:

Any day now.

PATHOLOGY

*T*here is healing because of suffering,
Renewal after being shattered.
Synthesis is born from analysis;
Light never unveils truth within light.

We ask *Why*, for there outlies a reason,
We ask *How*, for we examine a path,
We ask *When*, for tomorrow bears results,
We ask *Where*, for hope falls within range.

As numbers guide the healer's cure
And biopsies diagnose disease,
Prayer directs the spirit's course;
Searching within defines the soul.

A TOME OF FACES: IN A SURREAL MUSEUM

I am not obliged

to showcase my life's art

in this ceaseless, flowing exhibition hall,

once built for linked threads and letters,

where a wide circle of familiar strangers

can instantly view my curated creations.

I am not obliged

to unveil my guarded artifacts,

nor do I secretly hope

to kindle envy from vacant eyes,

within this museum,

> once ordained

> to bind hearts, to entwine lives,

> but which now unravels instead.

How many, in their hearts,

truly love the genuine relics

I have displayed?

Do they themselves feel obliged to

   react with a finger's touch,

      swipe the gleaming surfaces,

         mention what they ought to say, or

            post their own pleasant-only paintings?

Or do they echo the ticks of the clock

to simply

                              scroll past

the tube-like sculptured columns of others' lives?

And how many, in their minds,

would remember the true form of my art —

sophisticated, yet unseen —

among the flood of aspiring artists?

Though I may gain short nods from afar

(those, I do not need)

I alone

know its *unseen* beauty

and the narrative itself

behind the creation

of its unique, evolving profile.

Hence, I am not obliged

to prove it on display.

STICKERS

*C*lingy dry grass burrs

Spikes stick, stab and scar the heart.

Still, march through life's field.

REFLECTIVE FLOWER, OLD SONG

As this chrysanthemum turns sunward,
Light and shadow touch its face.
An intricate art piece—its beauty I admire.
Golden florets reflect feathery rays.

Easily pluck the flower, it will as easily die;
it lives on the earth, joined to its root.
Must I etch its sprouting portrait instead,
quietly watching it bend to bloom?

And like the flower's reflection,
a rediscovered tune starts to play.
With full heart I listen, gripped by a song,
compelling me to return to its day.

Its music brings tears,
lyrics scar and haunt.

Yet only now am I spellbound
by the nuances of its chant.

I have lost my voice;
I cannot croon anymore.
In my head, the song resonates,
never reaching an encore.

The flower's charm dazzles my eyes,
the song's echoes flood my ears—
each, reviving my worsening thirst
to jog the streets in wistful reverse.

Hence, I will
drag my eyes from the reflective flower,
clamp my ears against the old song,
wait until midnight passes,
escape before the hint of dawn,

and lie on hard, sturdy rock,

where I may finally script

tomorrow's play on the sky's sheets

in any imaginary way I see fit.

EMBRACE

I remember
the first time your fingers
curled beneath my drooly chin,
your other palm resting on my warm ears,
thumb stroking the bridge
between my eager eyes.

Intentions, love, and devotion—
these I gave you,
pure, simple, true.

Neither master
nor mere friend—
you're my home.
My family.

You made sure I've lived life's best:
a fraction of yours, a full one for me.

Cry, but don't fret.

A fog covers my vacant eyes
I whimper in the dusk
yet what I clearly see in brightness
is peace for both of us.

You gently nudge toward me
my cherished squishy toy,
lay beside my crusty nose
a favorite meaty treat
hoping
nostalgia, longing, and love
will miraculously
breathe life
back into my
heaving…
chest.

But all you can do now

is embrace me—

as you did when loud thunderclaps startled me—

and run your trembling hands

over my dull, disheveled fur,

while you gather the courage

to open the playpen door

and set me

free.

RITUALS

*P*uppets in an act, strings nodding heads
voices in a choir, mimes in a dance
when one does what another one does
and speaks the same, as in a trance.

Conditioned drones, not freeform fireworks
who equate orderliness with obedience
propriety with purity, rigor with reverence
who think holiness stems from stoic hindrance.

Sentiment adorns this garish masquerade—
traditionally prescribed vain rigmarole—
as it rises to the ceiling like censer smoke
which feels it can lift the heavy soul.

From Above, how does it look?

A manmade, brittle, stained-glass roof,

to hide and justify:

selfishness by sacrifice

pride by obeisance

immorality by dogmatism

injustice by acquiescence.

But in the cohesive motions of ten thousand,

a communal ceremony of celebration,

the *one* authentic, weeping heart

that humbly searches, offering no obligation—

for forgiveness, despite neither tribute nor tithe,

for love, while dressed in hideous, rotten hide,

for hope, though shadowed from white
candlelight—

is the Divine's exquisite find.

DESCENT

The malevolent curse of wilting

cuts off the old leaf

      from the tall tree's branch.

Thus begins the unrelenting journey

downward.

The guiding wind

      calls to the falling leaf:

      Look up!

But the leaf seals its eyes,

folds its arms,

gates its heart

descends,

resting in the playful air.

The compassionate wind

steadies the shaken leaf,

wafting it with careful might

yet the leaf refuses

to grasp those cradling arms,

sinks in its own comfort, continues its

descent,

and falls, at last,

to the unyielding earth.

On the ground—

       Forever bound?

The doomed leaf finally knows, whimpers,

then pleads,

cries out!

to the ever-present wind

and is lifted back

up—

a new leaf

upon the branch.

PATHS TO A SINGLE END

Which path shall I take at this point
     where ends the carefree way,
Where one road splits into many,
     each path luring me astray?
Uneven trails, narrow and broad,
     now gleam, some strewn with gold
Yet beyond lie quagmires, feared even
     by trekkers hardened by the road.

What perils wait, where many have fallen:
     if only I could know!
The sands where troubled paths sink:
     if only they would show!
Whether curving, straight, or steep,
     for now, I cannot tell,
Yet I must choose where to start before
     the dreaded winter spell.

Which path to take is mine to ponder;

to which should I give ear?

The legends ripened by travelers,

the painful vision of a seer,

The counsel of the unseen Wind,

the cynics foretelling doom,

The stirrings of my soul and reason,

To discern what brings misfortune?

Yet should I seek fortune,

there are countless paths to victory.

Though diverse are the tracks that lead me,

what matters is who I shall be,

What calls me, what shapes me—

on one road my journey I spend.

Now I choose the way of my heart,

among all paths to a single end.

SABBATH

$\mathcal{L}$et me pause awhile,

to see the blossoming fields

on my next turn to the left.

Let me gaze at them and run through them

and know where their roots lie.

Allow me a peaceful moment to enjoy

every final detail

that enthralls these mortal senses.

I want to take my remaining time

to solemnly sit upon velvet hills,

communing with the infinite, sublime sky,

surrounded by fragrant lavender and free bluebonnets,

while uplifting drafts rush by;

to absorb the sunlight's warmth

and to steep it in needy grasses,

pushing away anxious dew to the clearing's side

as I savor,

with heavy, lingering thoughts,

this momentary bliss—

but a foretaste

of what is eternally mine.

And after this brief resting moment

I shall,

once more,

plod along the lonely, empty, dusty road

that awaits me home.

CREED OF THE LIGHTED BEACONS

While the elements rage,

the quest goes on

to have what is needed,

to be what is rare,

in a changing, shattered world.

We desire to stand out,

to be strong,

to hold conviction,

to bend not as the world does,

to walk the sound paths,

to earn wisdom from Above.

It is steadfast, steeled faith that holds us,

that strengthens the will

against all turmoil and charm,

that holds the soul in rectitude

while winds turn and the earth trembles.

It is warm, beckoning hope that keeps us

treading toward the unfathomable

with our flares undying,

glancing neither around

nor behind

at the false beacons that eventually die.

It is luminous love that moves us

to resolute dedication,

belittles fear,

and inspires a

loyalty that keeps us true.

We know where we stand

and stand fast, we will,

upright, unwavering, replete;

like the firmament, unyielding

like the diamond, enduring.

For out of the dark mist,

our lighted pillars

across the world

shine forth

with silvery rays.

"Lighted Pillar"

Dubai, United Arab Emirates

THE LADY AND THE CALL

The Lady and the Call:
two crowns, young seeker,
your heart embraces.

Behold the remnants,
relics of other lives.
They have mastered the turns
of both earth and sky.
Yet your choice, your destiny,
is but one brittle flake
to be struck surely, only once.

Shall you make the sweet mount your home?
Or shall you heed your heart's other half,
to enter the silver portal
and cross into the great star's cradle?

Stay, and never again soar.

Soar—and never return.

Look nonetheless farther, *deeper*;

peer into the

quiet

space

of truth

beyond the mountain and the star

beyond the Lady and the Call

And find how to truly live.

ONE LAST

*D*ream
fulfilled —
it's you
in the violet eve
in the mirror you hold for me;
I do not see myself
but you

I return to you;
seeing you lie asleep
lips parted,
head dreamless,
heavy upon the pillows
is just a miracle
that transcends what poets and oracles
have inscribed on their linens

when every full moon

steals your light to lend to the moment,

I will gather star beams, return to you

when shadows bind me

by the endless mocking of earthly fears,

I will break the ties, return to you

and after I trespass infinity's gates

and walk back to this night,

I will join you, return to you

in this final, enduring adventure,

now.

ASCENT

*H*igher still
did I lift my widened gaze
ablaze with grandiose visions
as my climb to the top unfolded.

My chipped blade of grit
survived cutting through rocks of fear
tattered cloak
held against disenchanting winds
broken spectacles
struggled to grasp the sight of
boundless, untangled lights—
ever-shining stars—
to which the soul
wearily raised its arms.

Despite the end still lying unforeseen

I paused and turned back to my journey past:

Paths curved, broke—disappeared,

seemed forever impossible

      inclined

   steeply

treacherous

yet the journey proved a steady ascent;

I had never trekked alone.

I was losing the day as I did my reason,

then the gentle Voice reminded me,

"Your pace is your own,

but the incline is not."

And I was not where I had been, I saw.

Although I had ascended, I wanted to climb still:

To struggle, stumble but never leap down.

Higher still, in time

I will go.

I will stop.

Rest.

Move on.

At the perfect pace intended for me.

"*Serene*"

Wyoming, USA

Dear Reader, thank you for accompanying me in this poetic journey: from cheerful sunshine, through stark shadows, to serene rest under the starlight of hope.

Before this chapter—and this book—ends, I want to leave you a little prayer-poem that points us back to the Source of all hope, the true, ever-present Light of the world.

MEDITATION: A PRAYER FOR STARLIGHT

Should I fly too high above the winds

Gently draw me back to the earth;

I could not have viewed canyons from clouds

Without the wings You lent me.

Should I dive too deep below the waters

Grant me the moon's true pearl:

That I rise above the surface to seek

Those who need love as I do mine.

Let me, then, fix my gaze on starlight

Beyond the lake's deep shadows;

Your gentle ripples never cease

Steering me—to where I belong.

Acknowledgments

First and above all, to God, for giving me strength and hope despite the challenges of fulfilling this dream.

To you, the reader, for taking some of your precious time to read my book. Your support means the world.

To my teachers: Thank you for fueling my lifelong love for writing; you always come to mind.

To my parents, relatives, and friends, for your priceless encouragement and inspiration. This book would not exist without you.

To my wife: Thank you for your unwavering love and support, especially for your calm and patient presence while I am lost in thought with my computer. It means more than you know. I love you.

To my co-creators, Zacharie and Zephanie, whose earnest drawings brilliantly interpret each chapter of the book's journey. I am proud of you.

Thank you to everyone who has been a part of this journey. I look forward to sharing more explorations with you.

About the Author

Eufe Tantia, Jr. is a medical laboratory scientist by profession
and a fan of science fiction TV/films. He relates, through his
writing, the rigor of clinical analysis to the careful scrutiny of
life's vast nuances. An optimist by nature, he enjoys the
challenge of detecting hopeful notes within cynical and
pessimistic viewpoints—a juxtaposition that fuels his creative
engine.

Dividing Untangled Light: Verses of the Finite Heart is his debut
poetry collection. He currently lives with his wife and children
in Texas.

He can be reached by email at: etjr.poetry@outlook.com.